Sports et plein air
Livre de coloriage

Coloring Pages for Kids

Coloring Pages for Kids
An imprint of Ciparum LLC

Sports et plein air Livre de coloriage
© 2017 Ciparum LLC
All rights reserved.
ISBN-10:1-63589-355-0
ISBN-13:978-1-63589-355-7

Coloring Pages for Kids

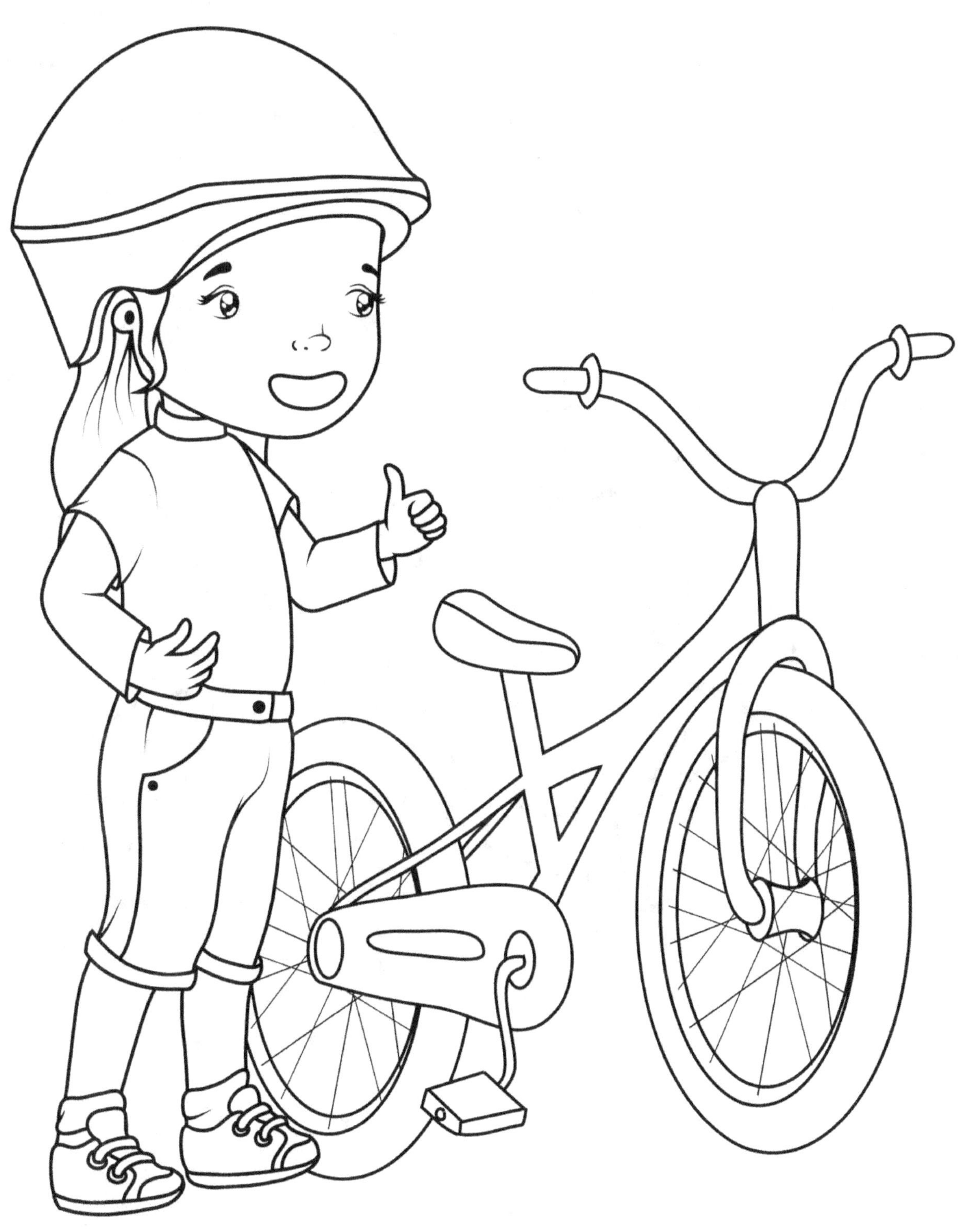

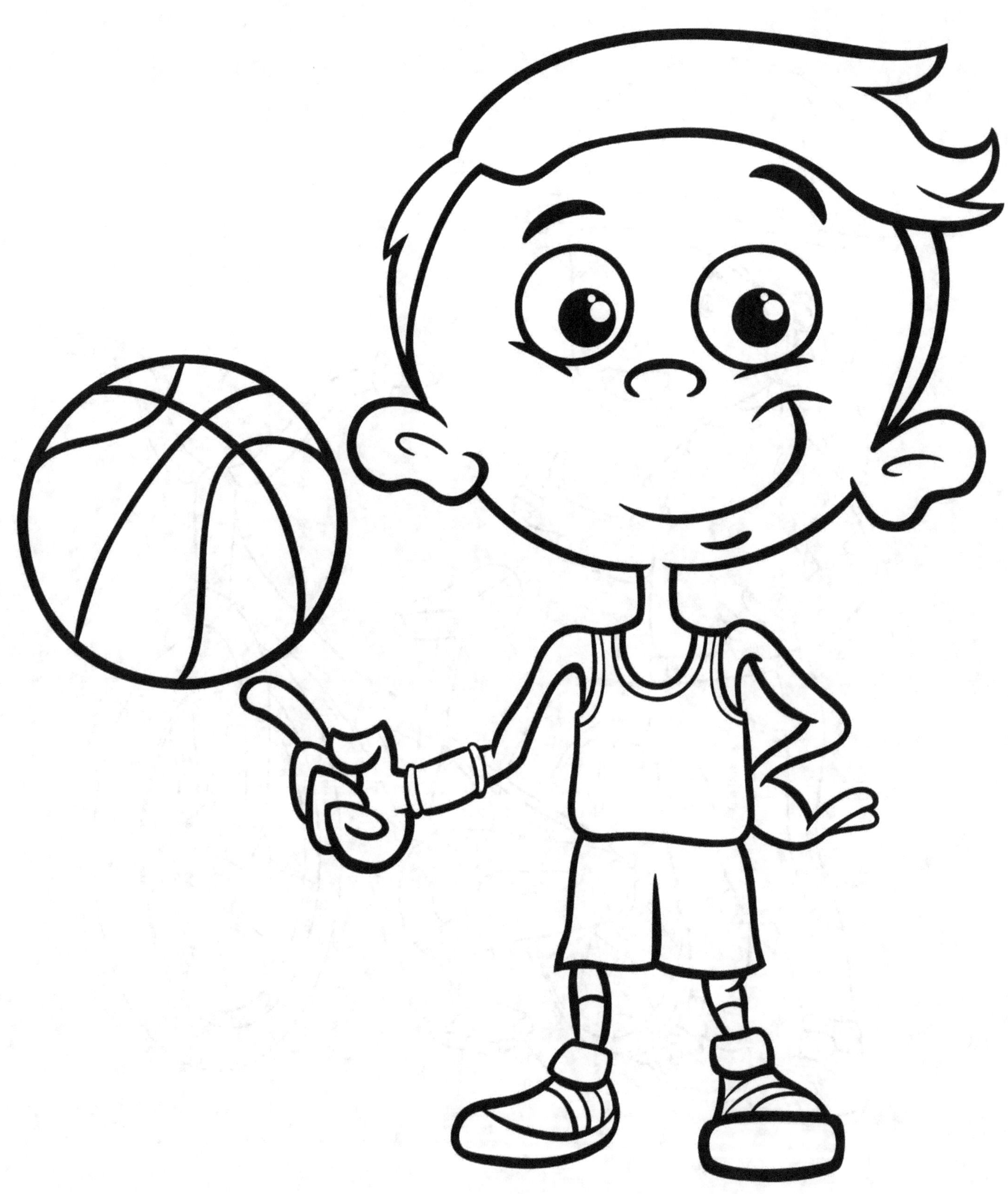

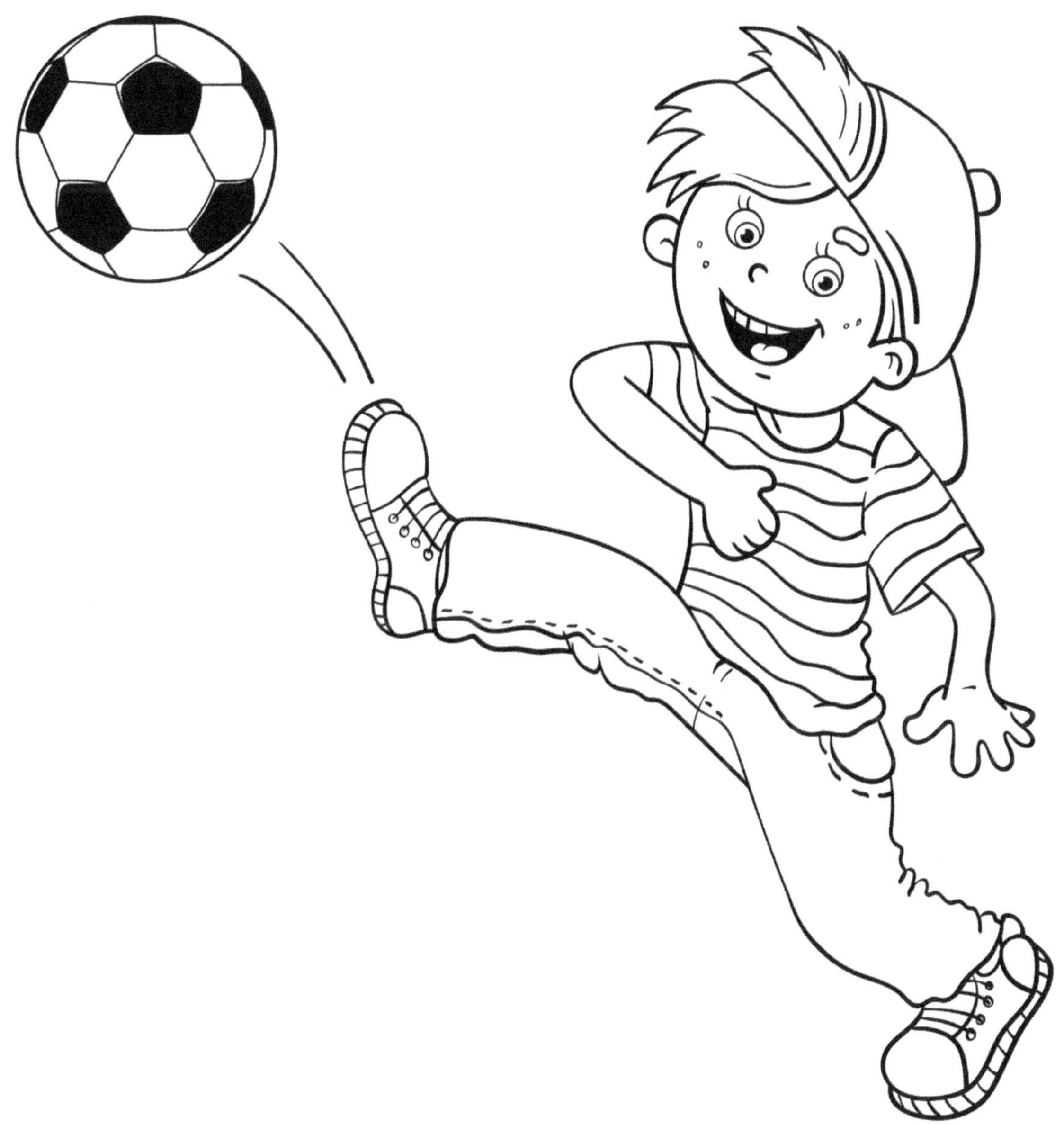

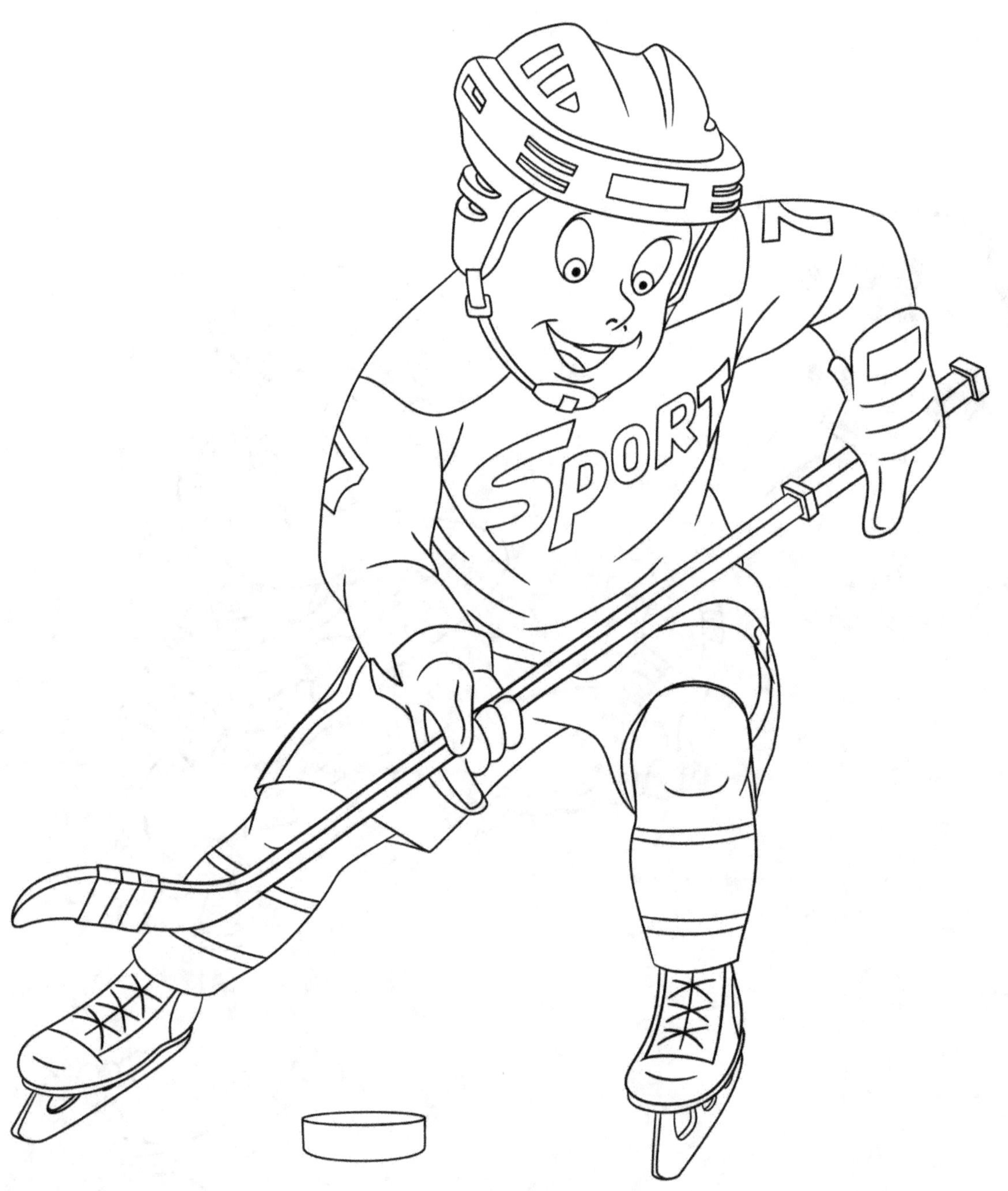

SPORT

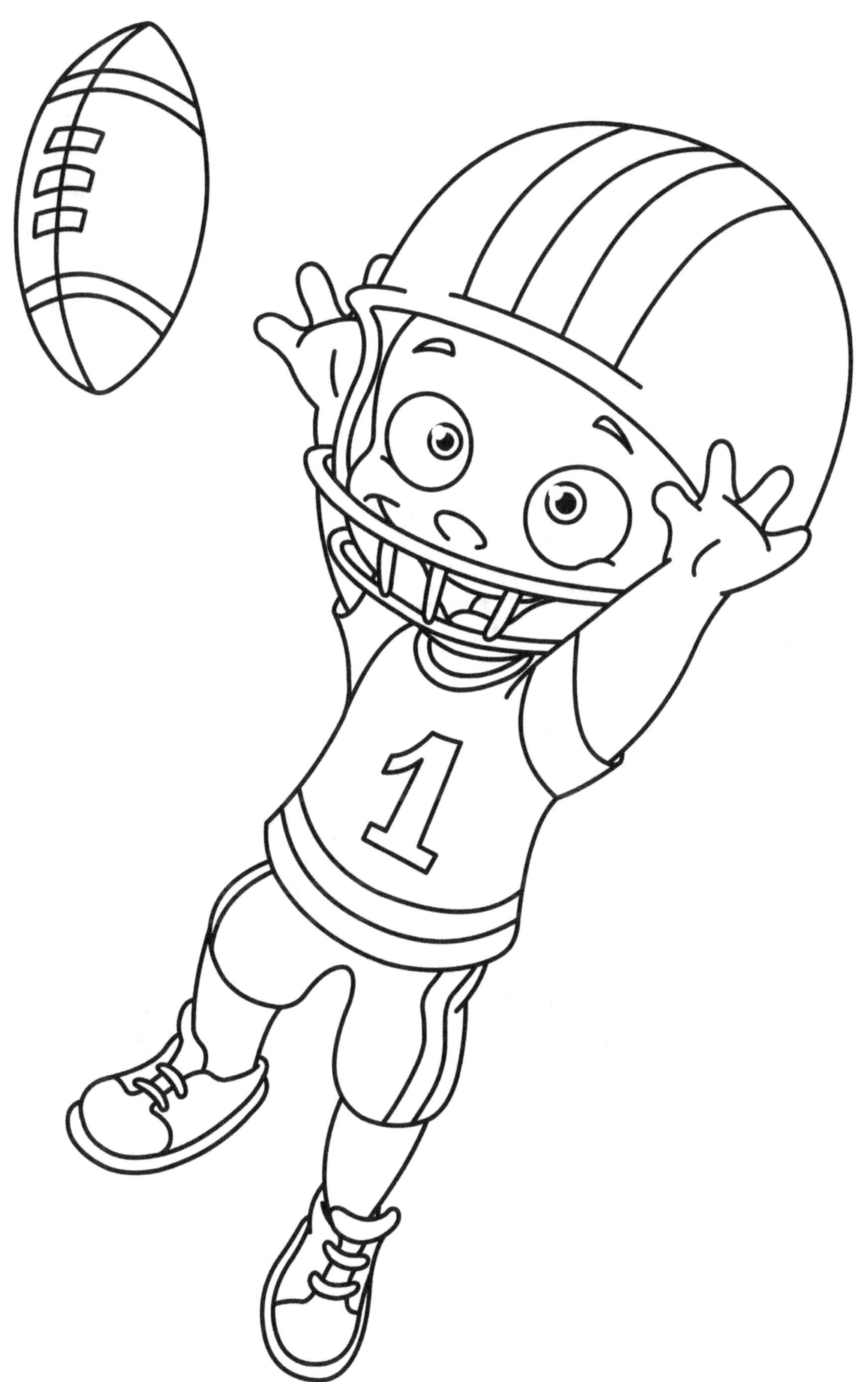

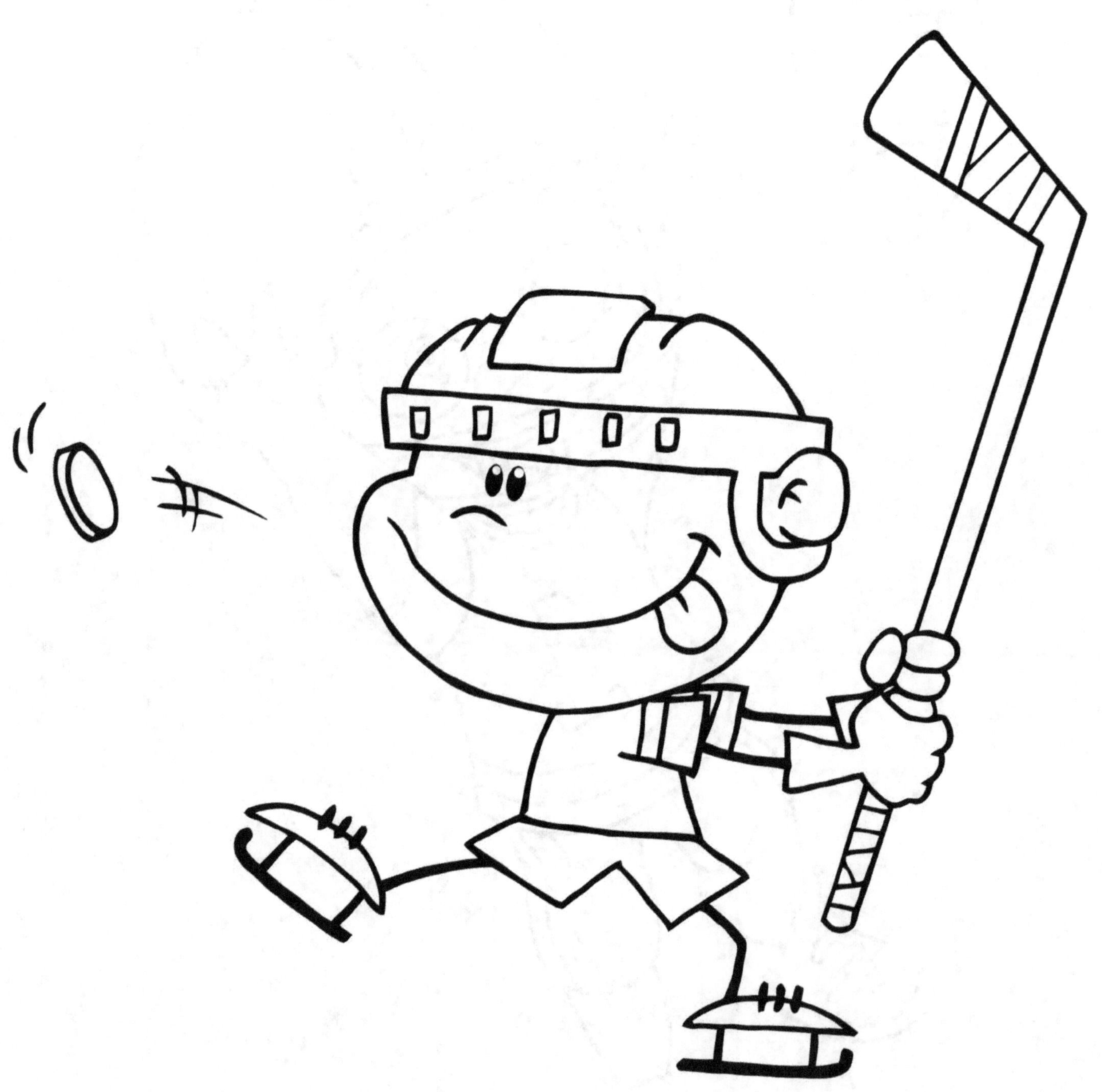

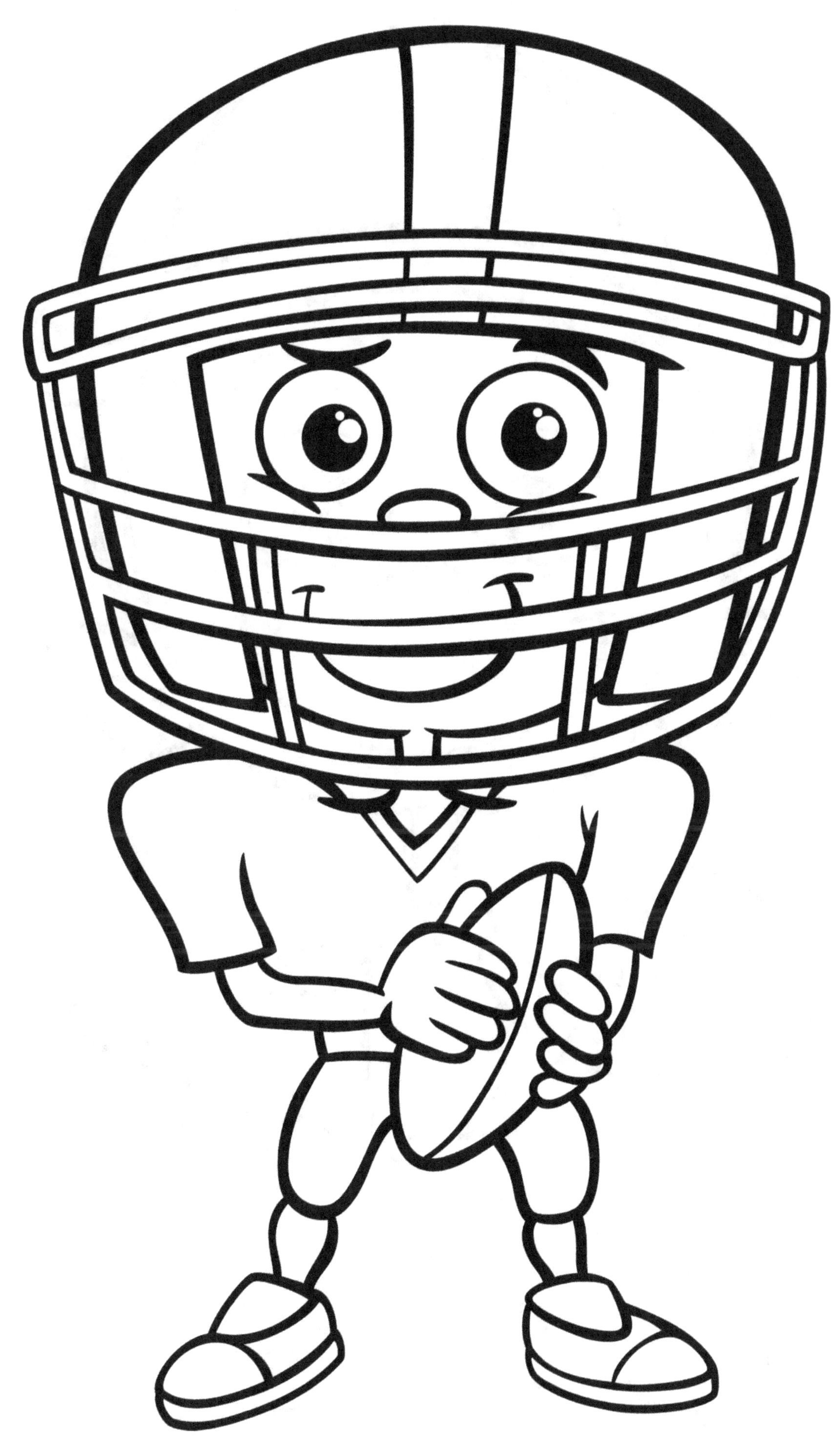

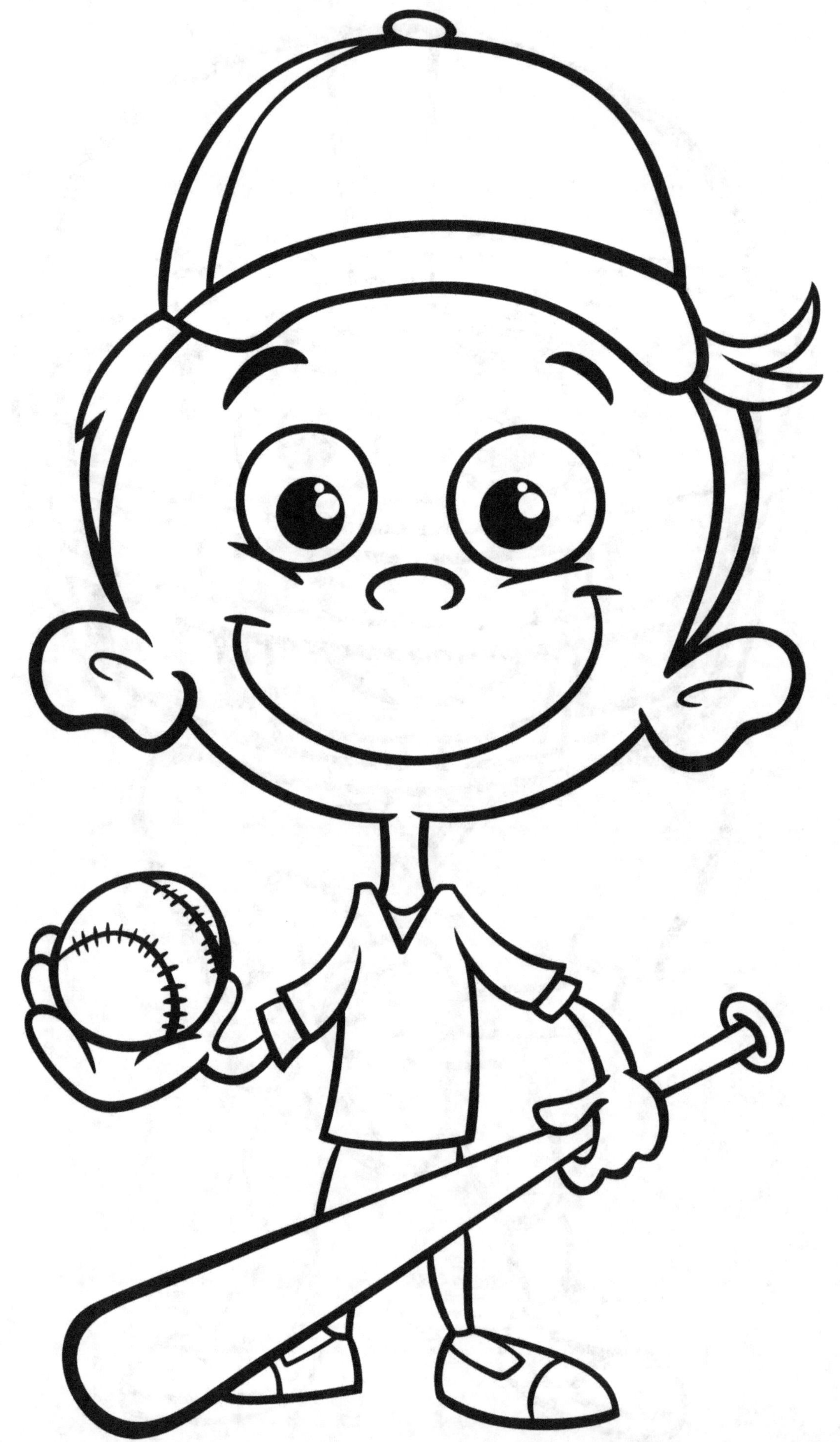

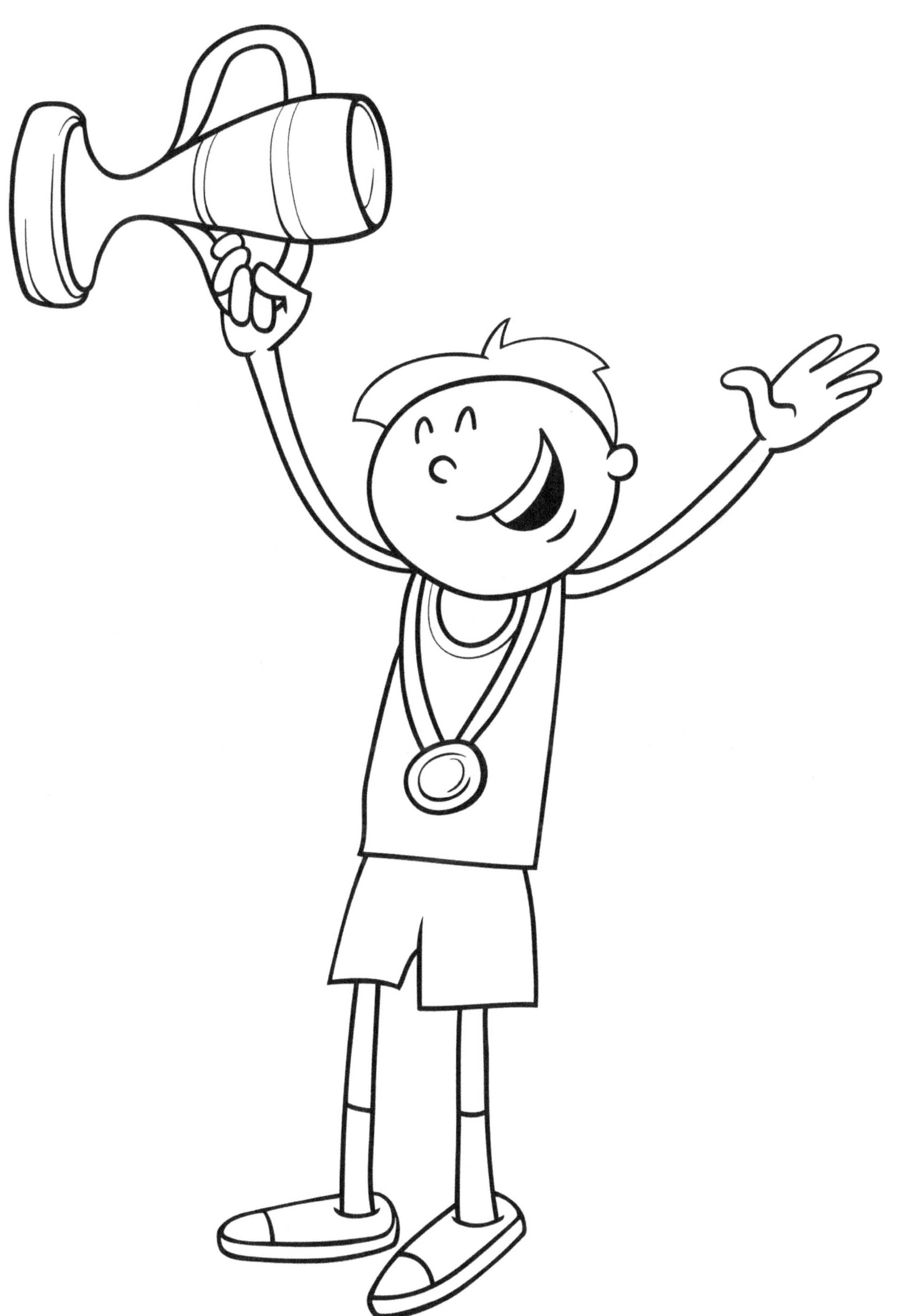

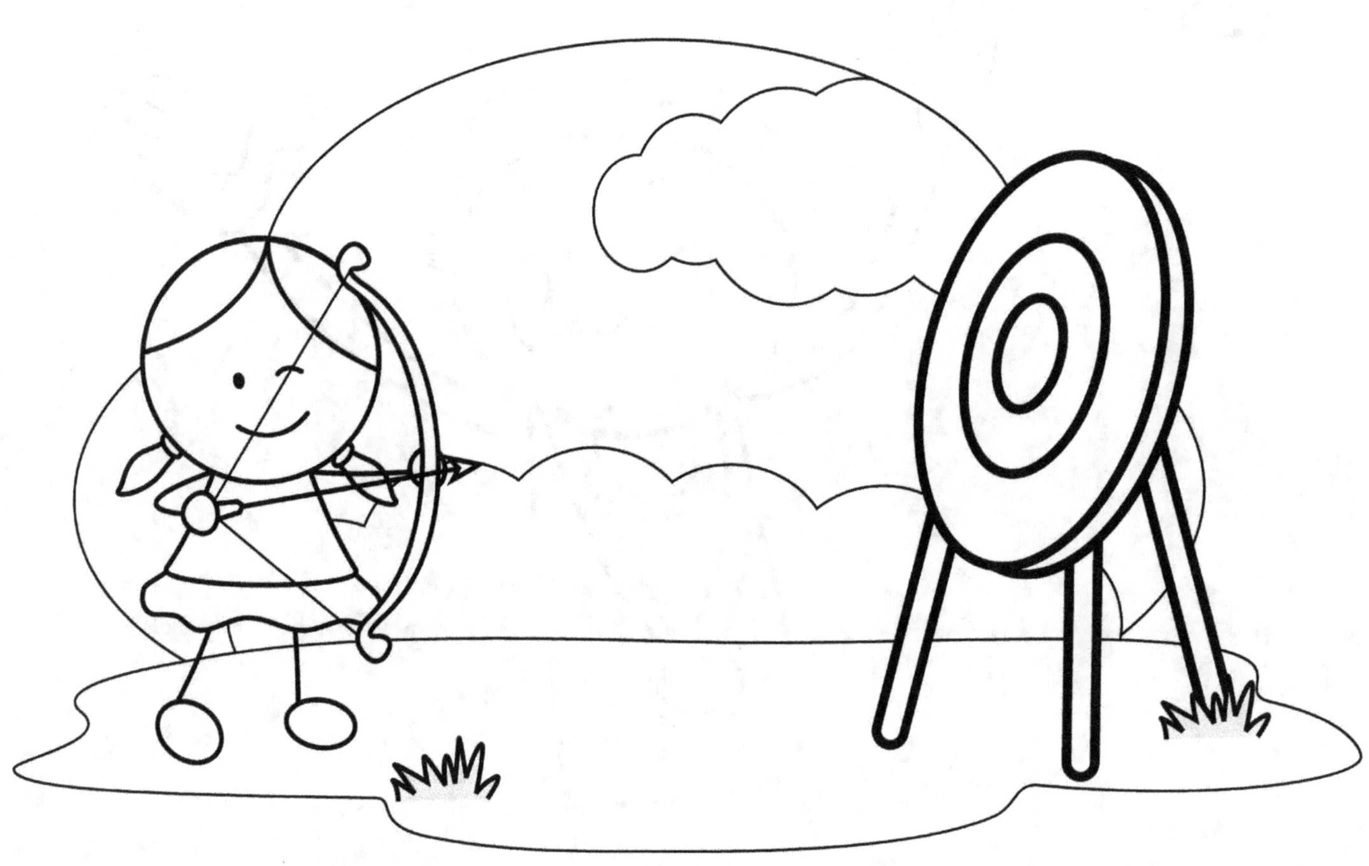

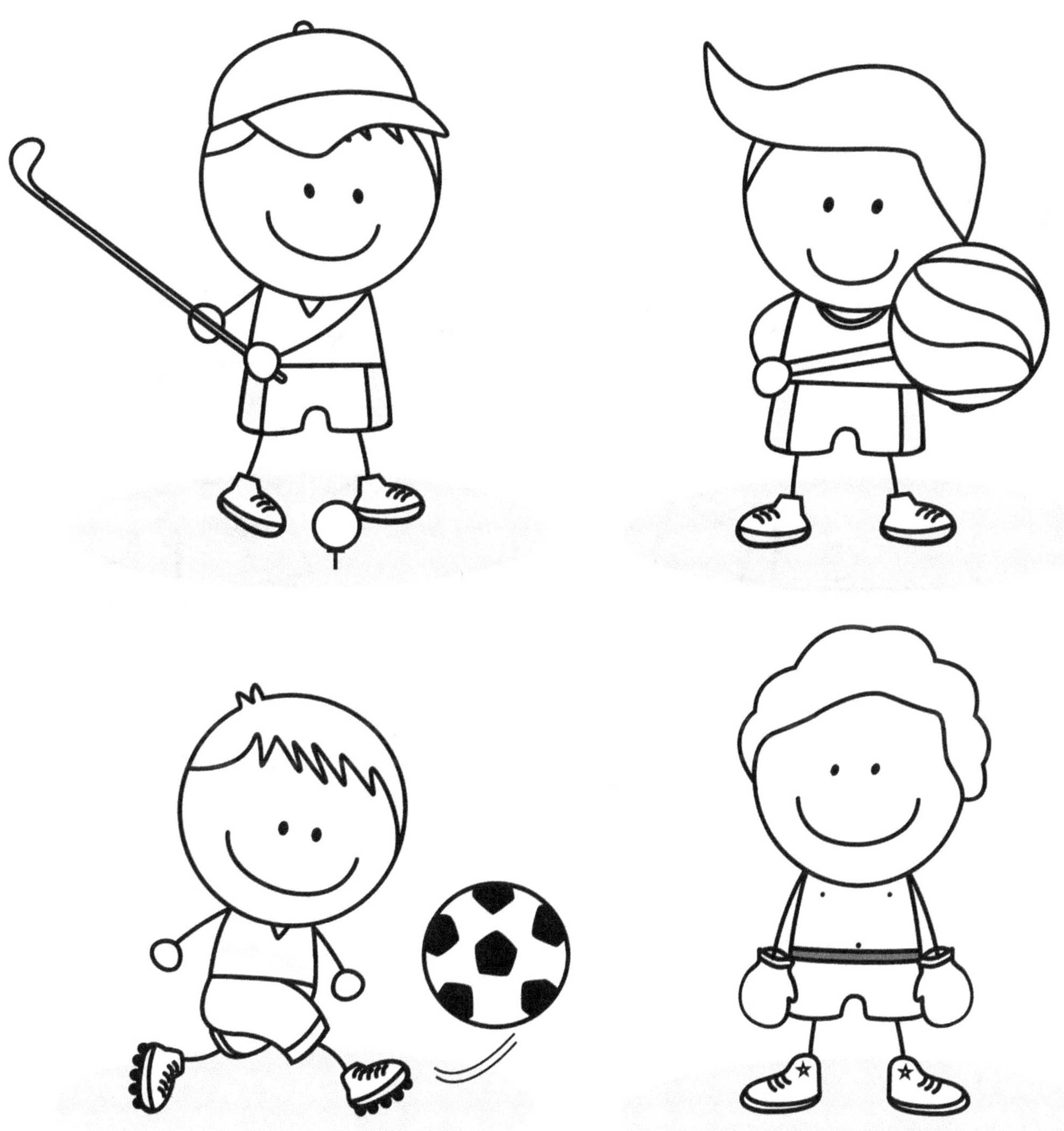

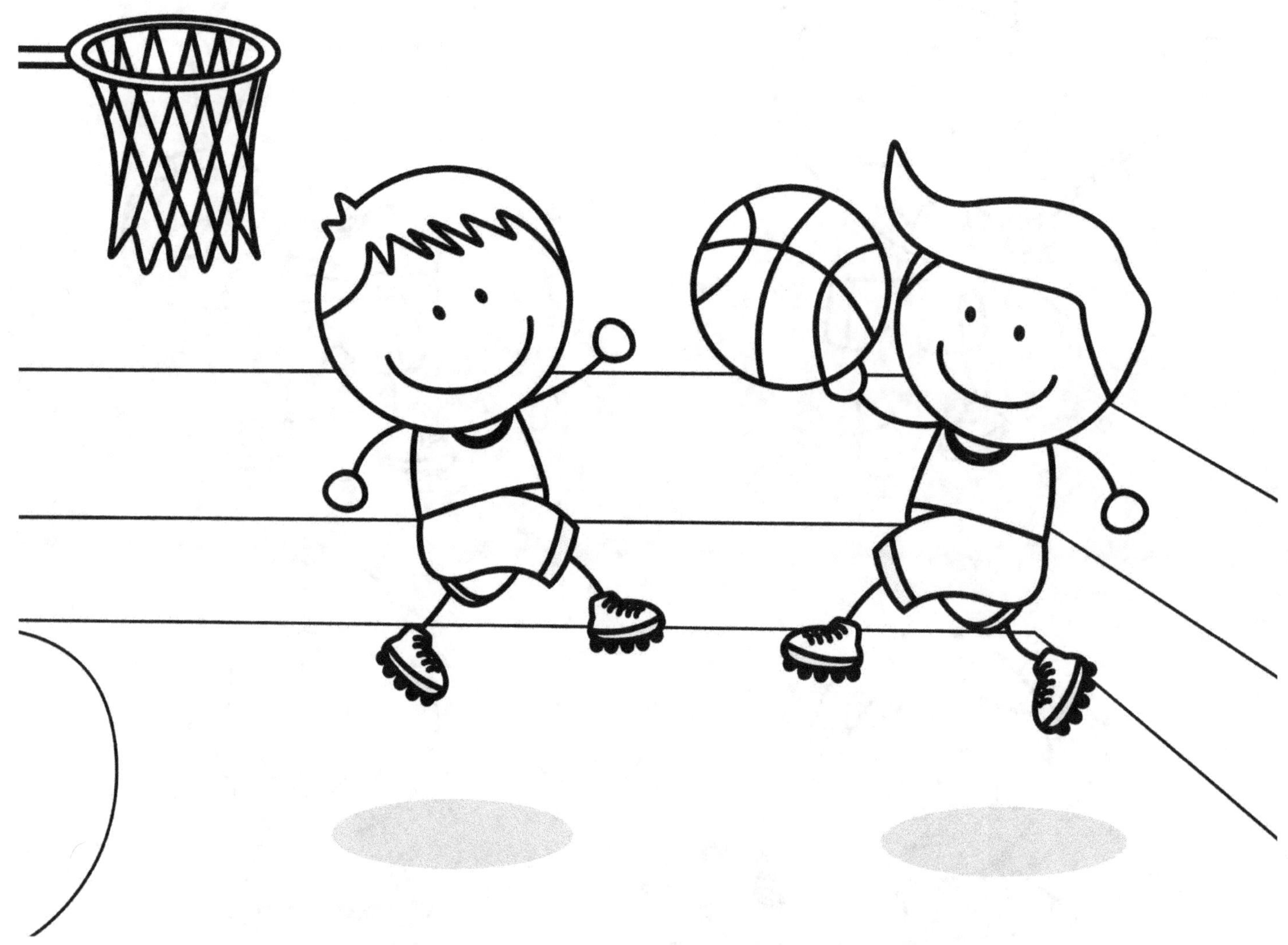

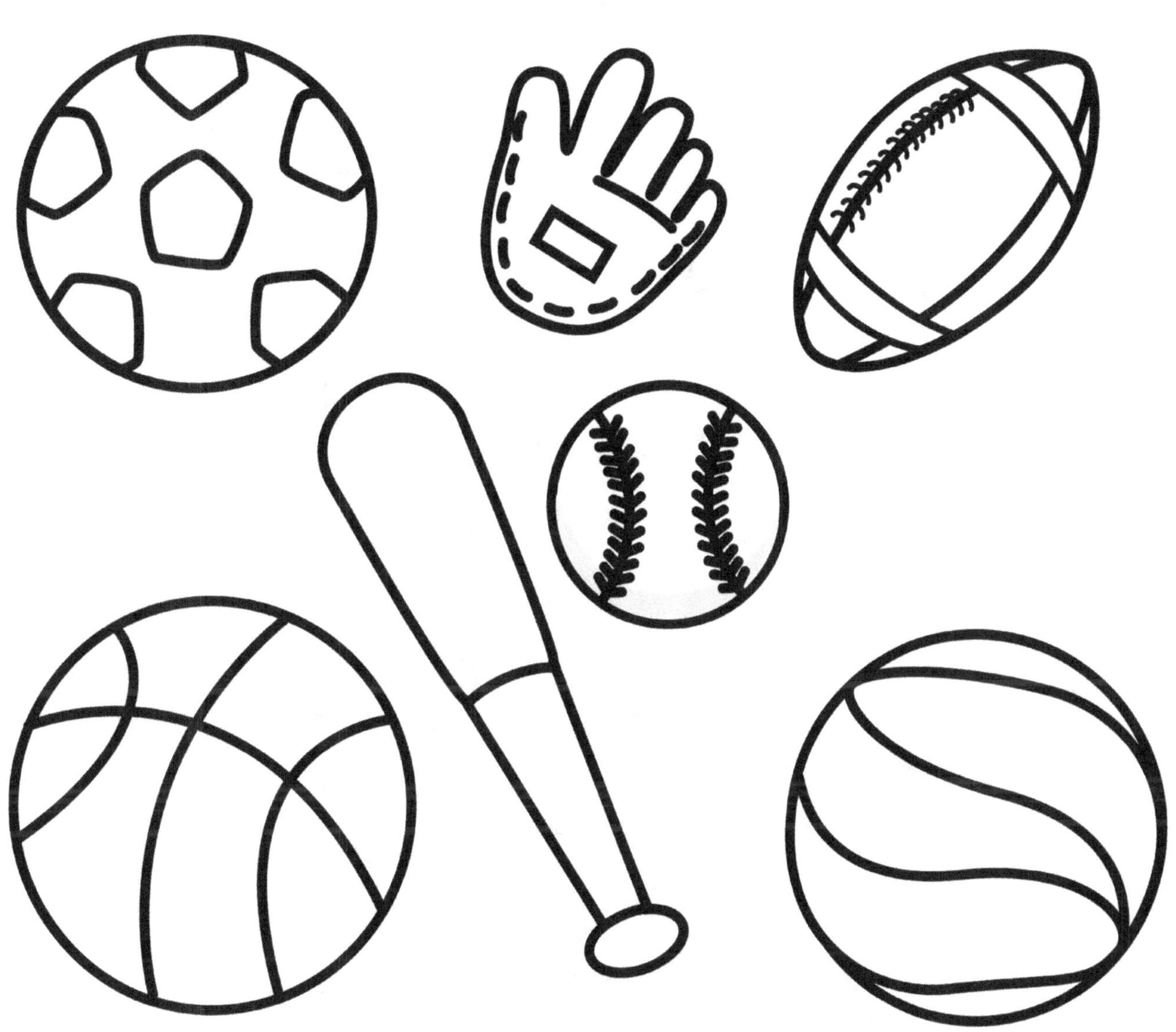

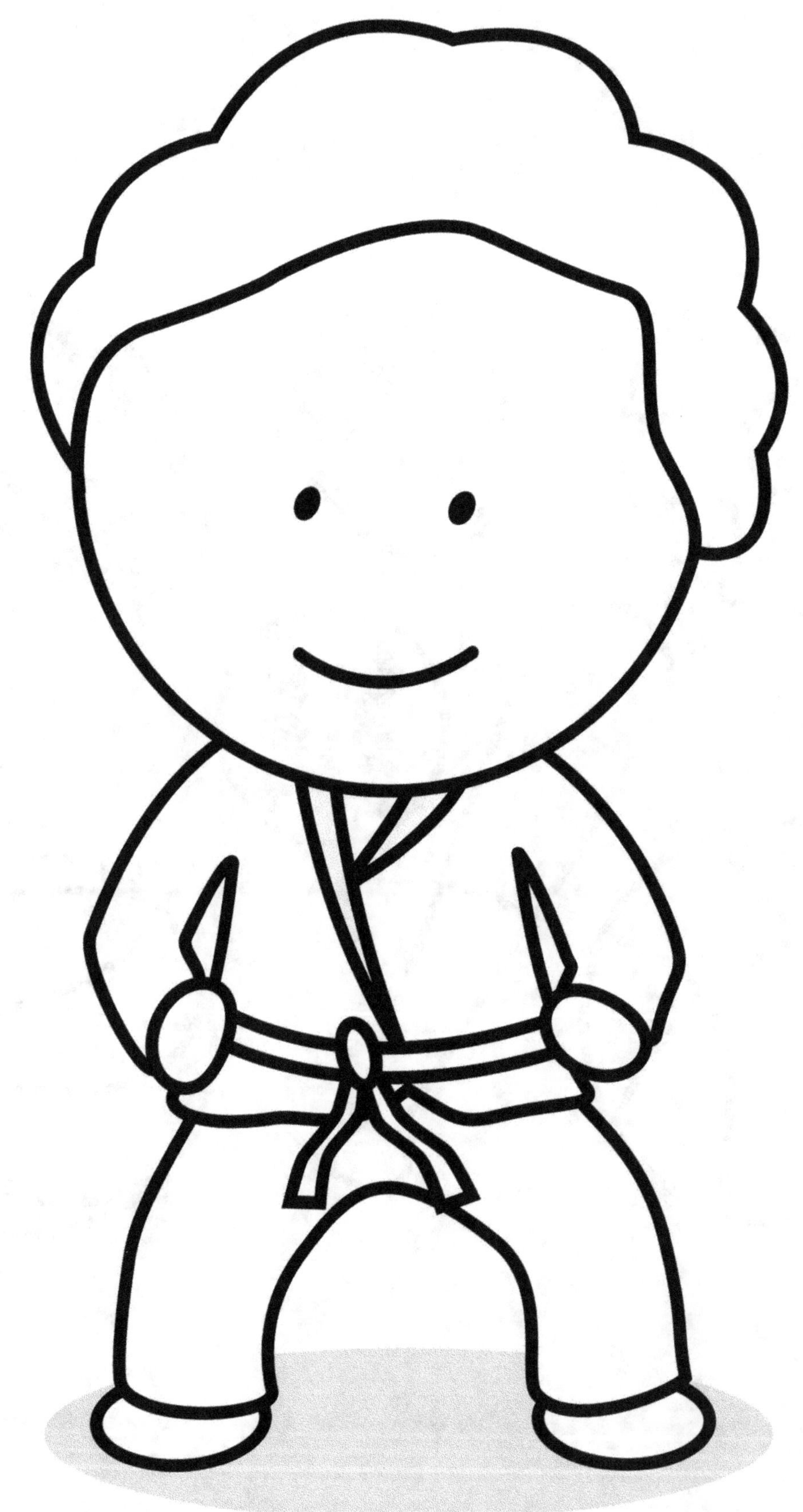

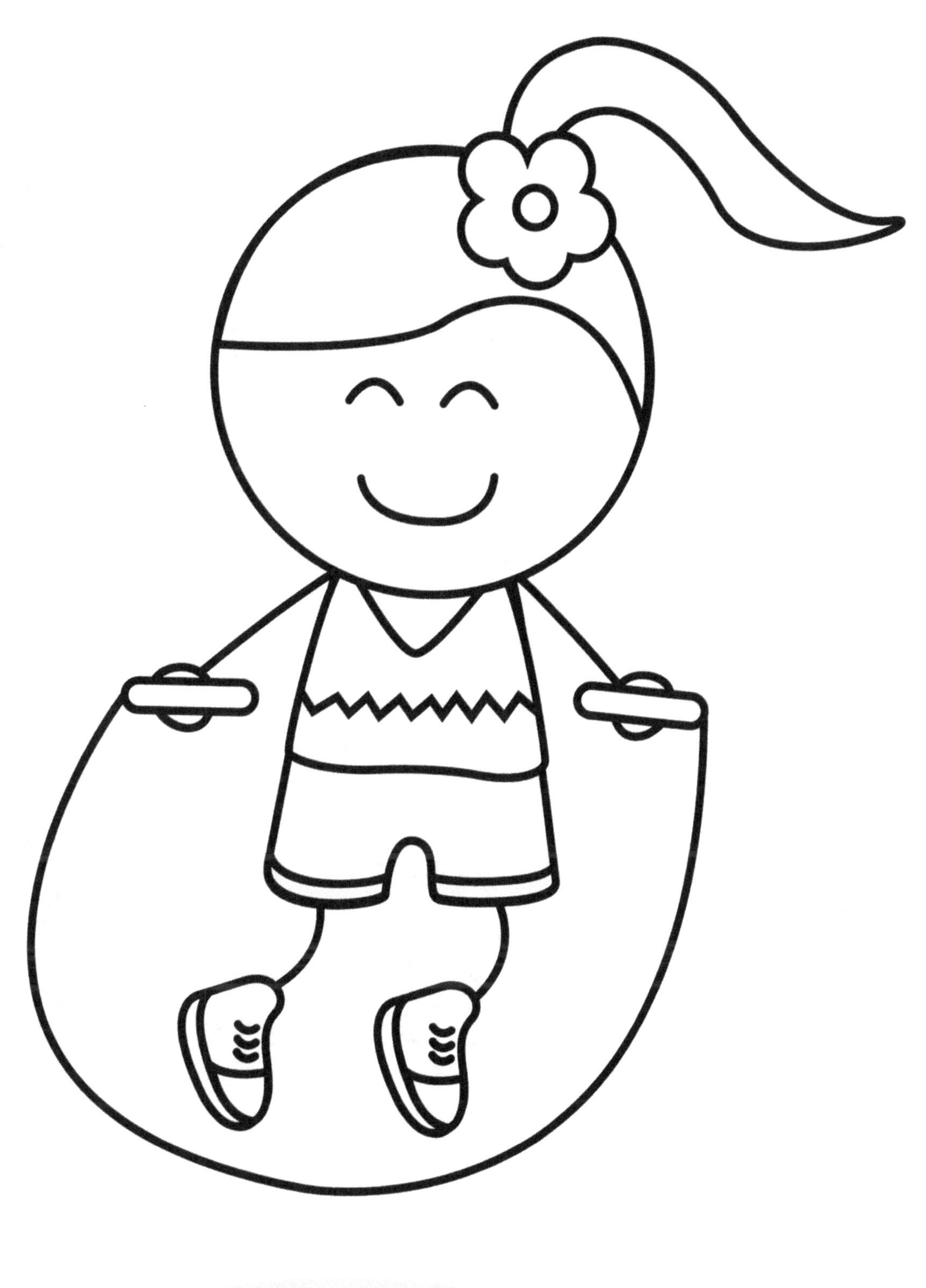

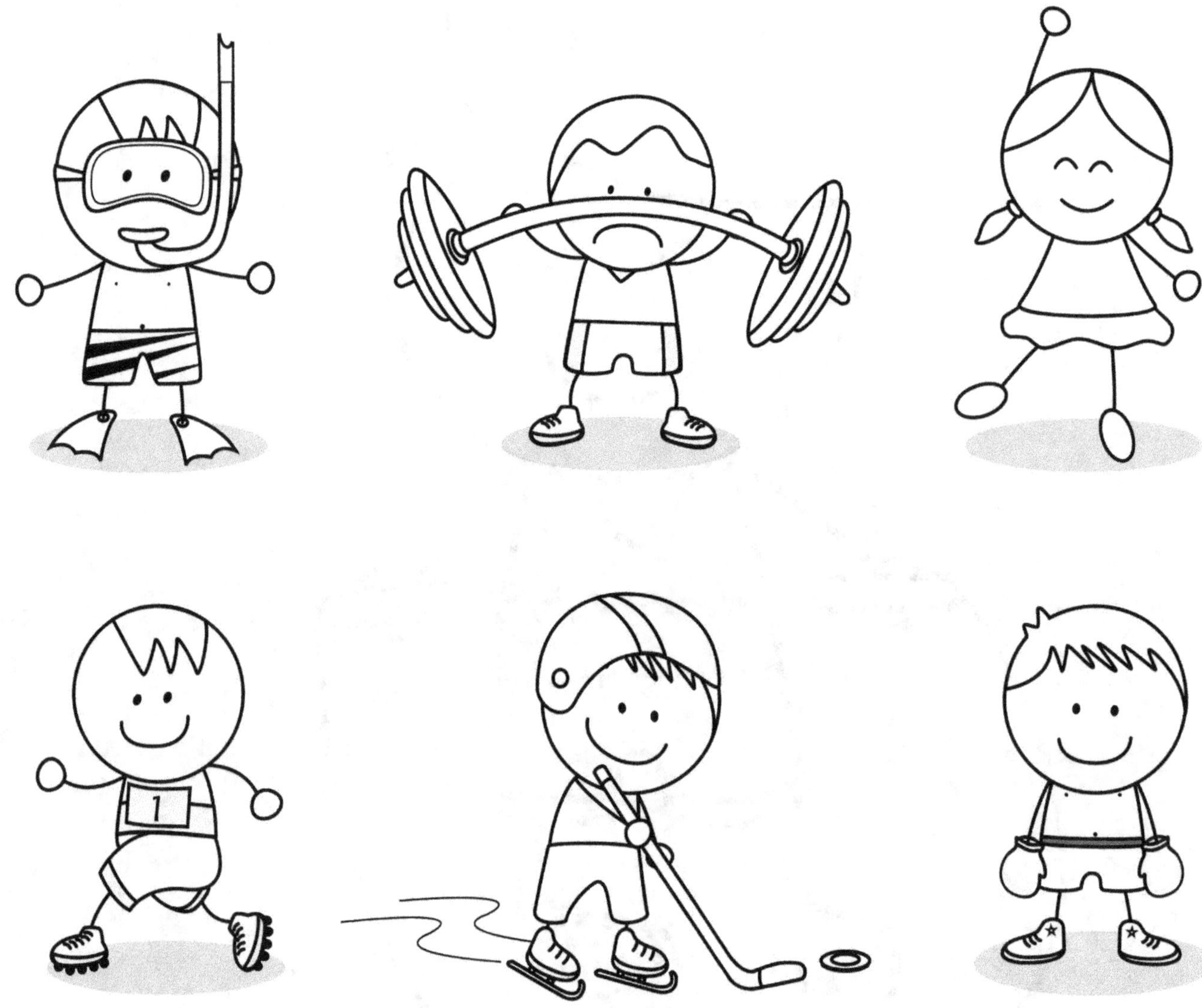

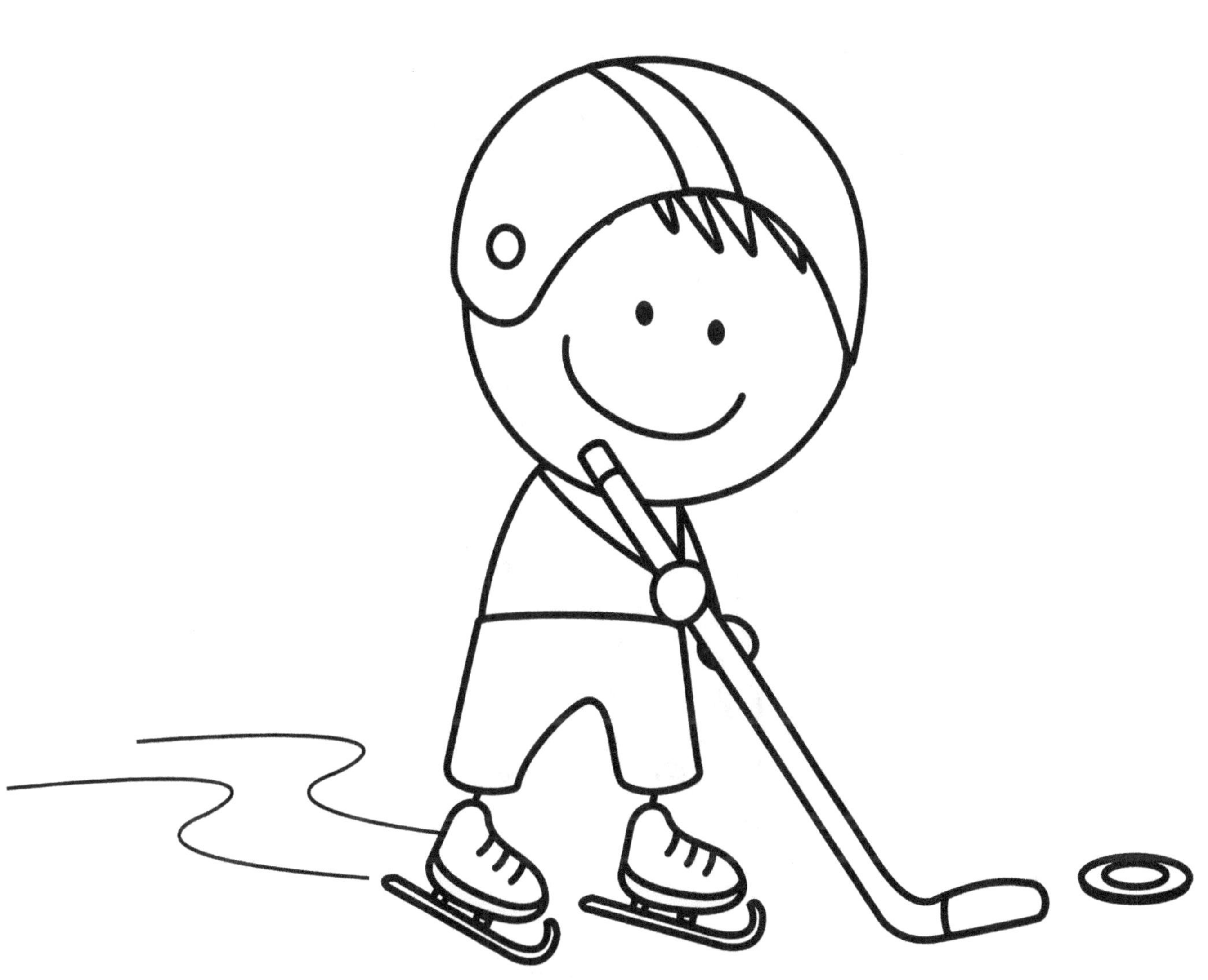

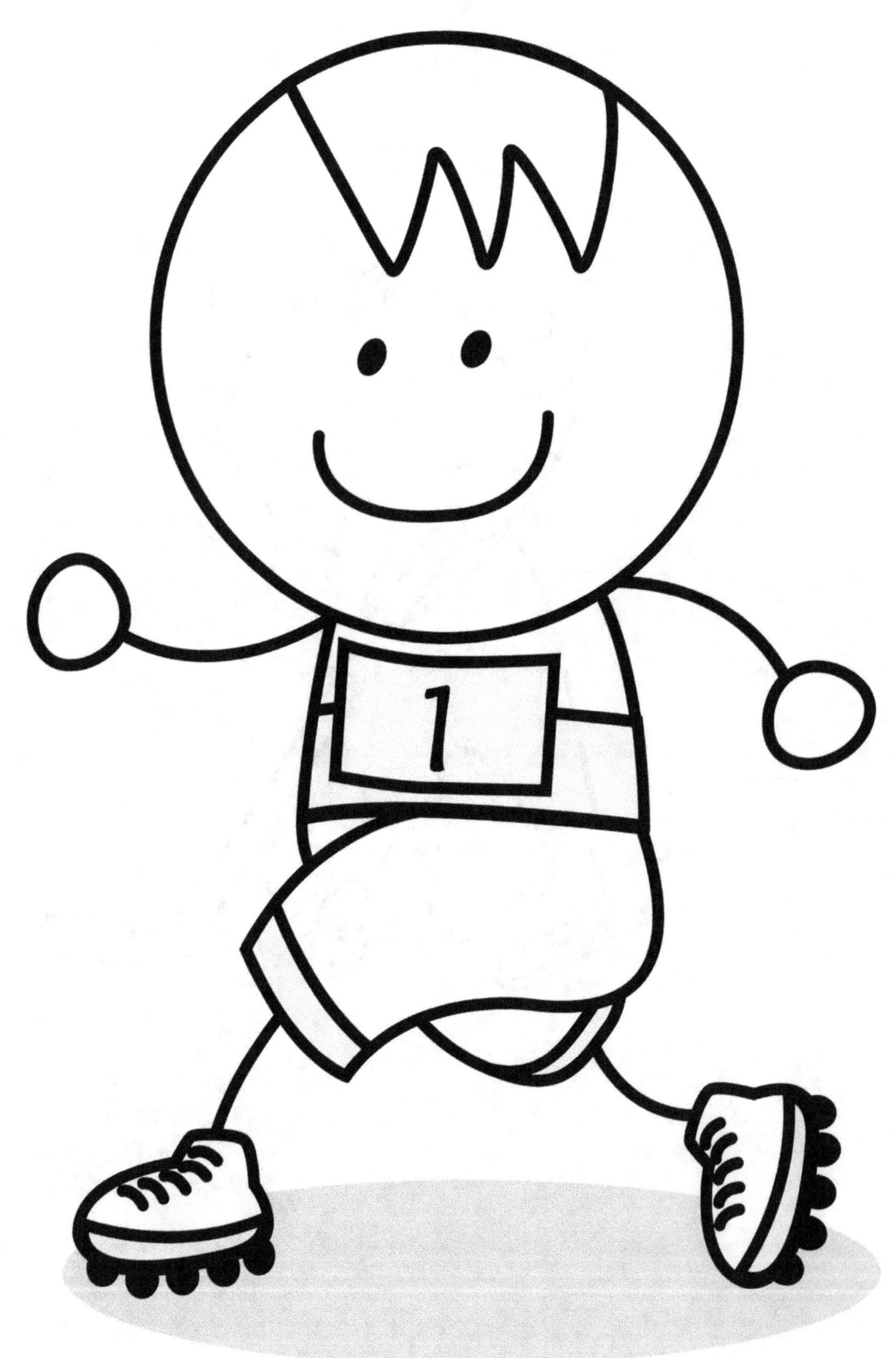
1

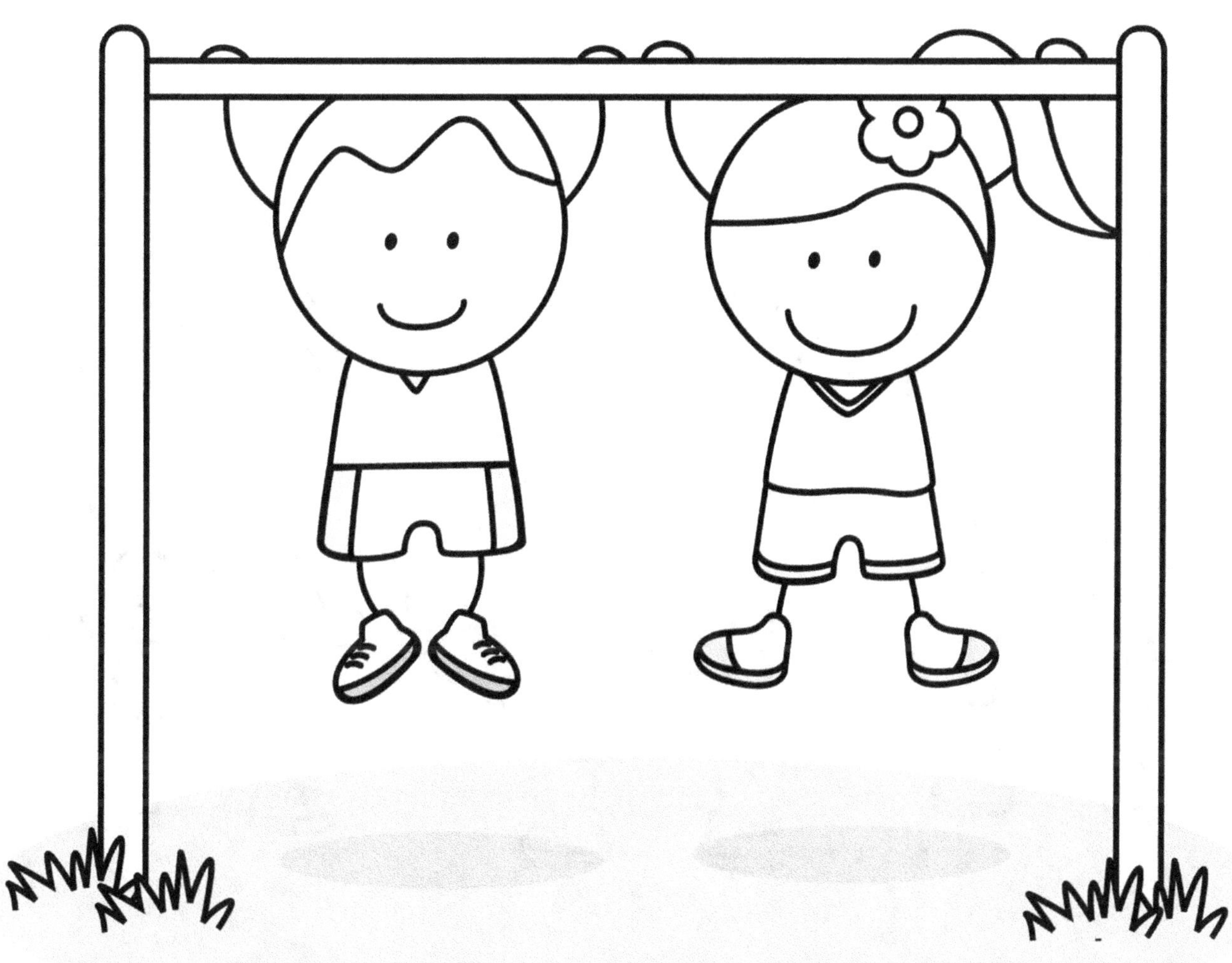

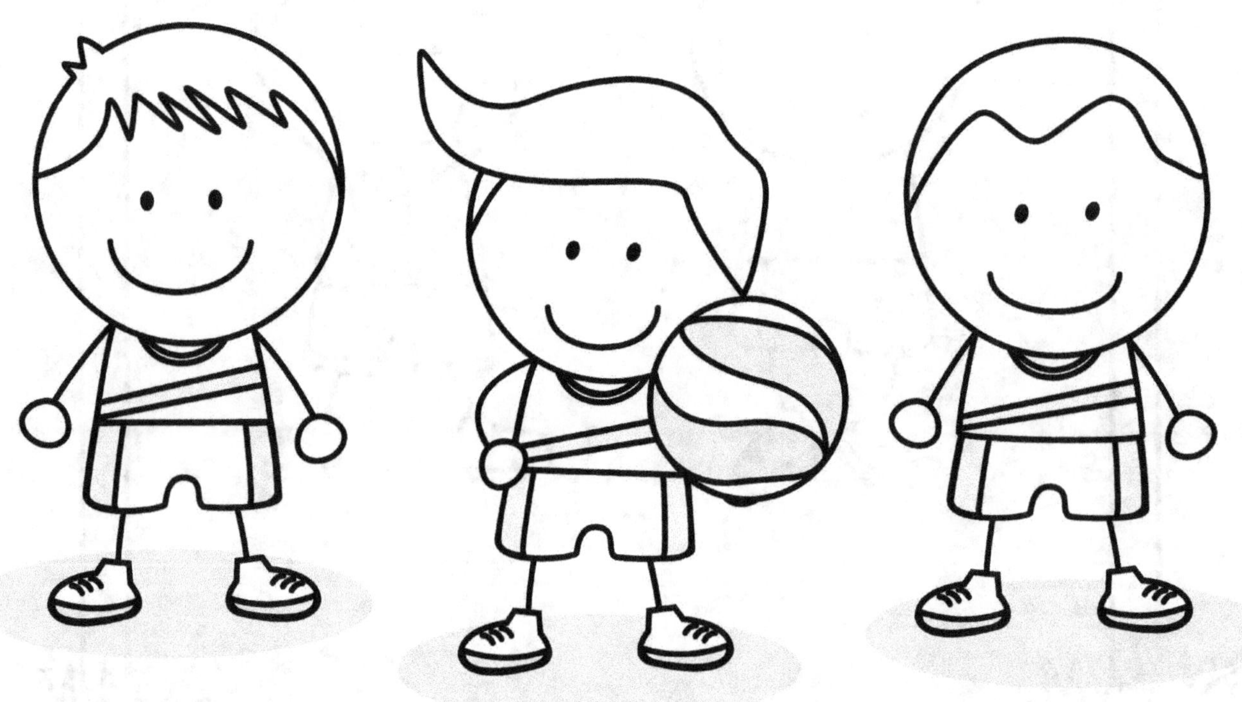

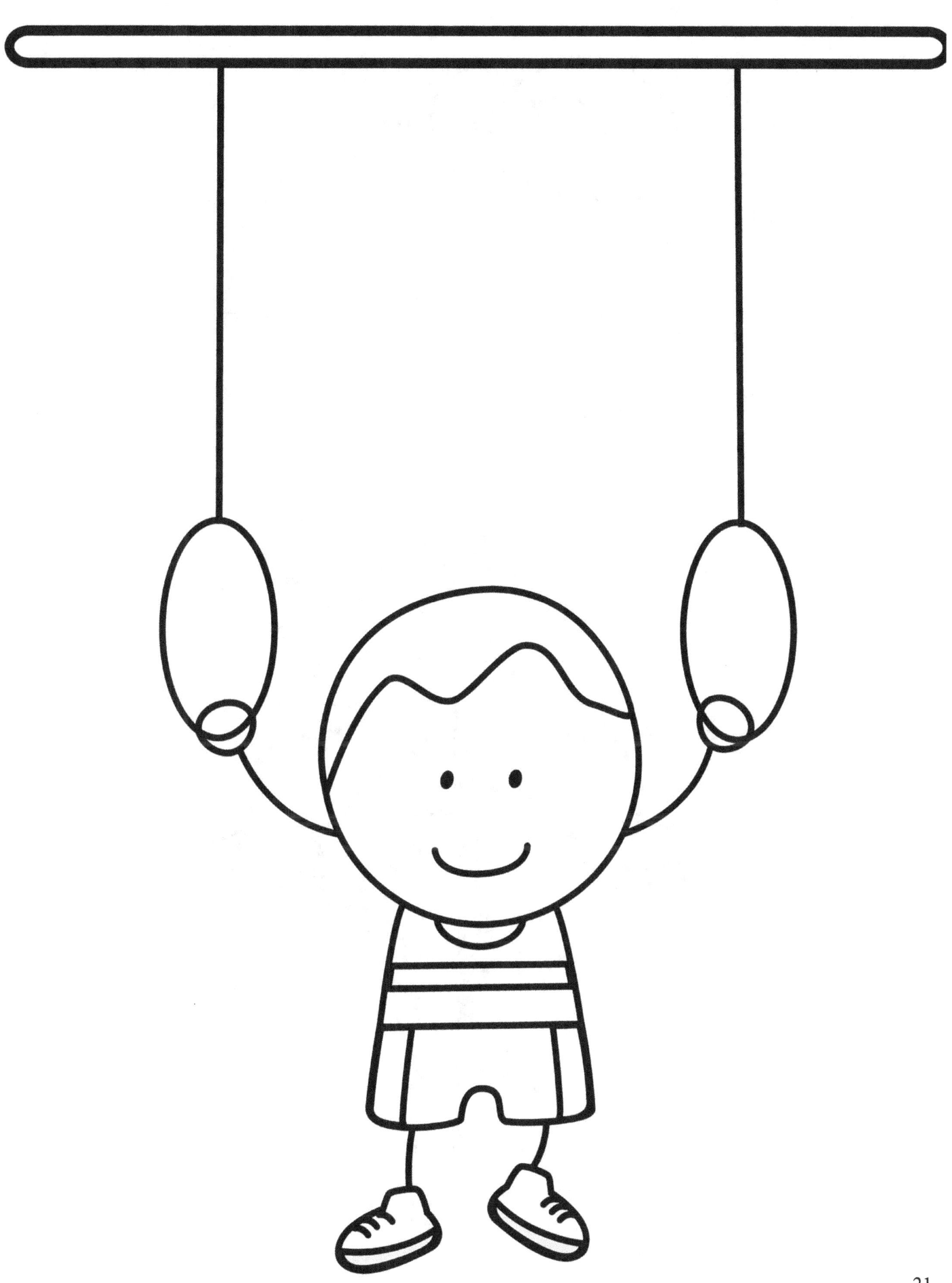

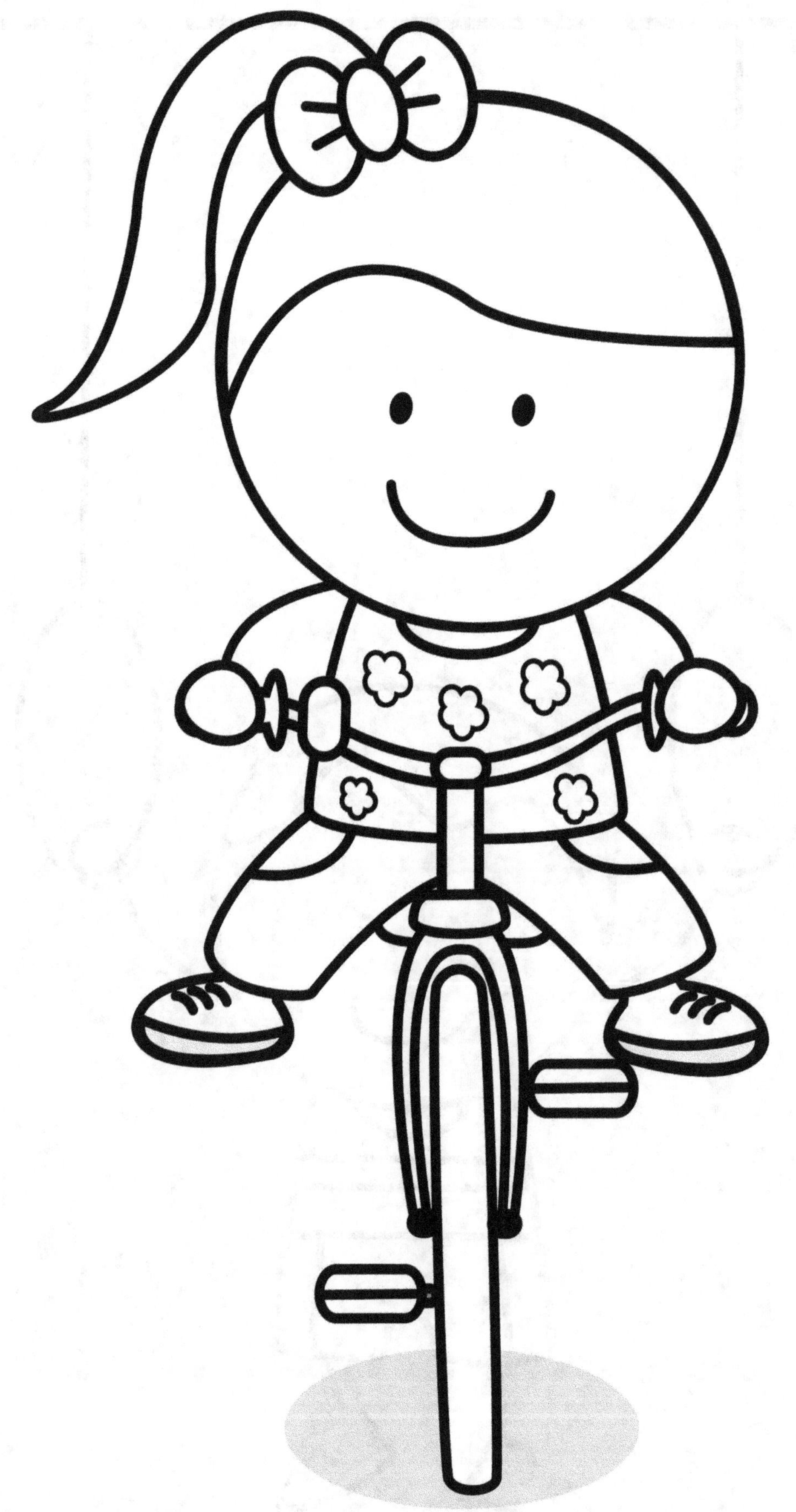

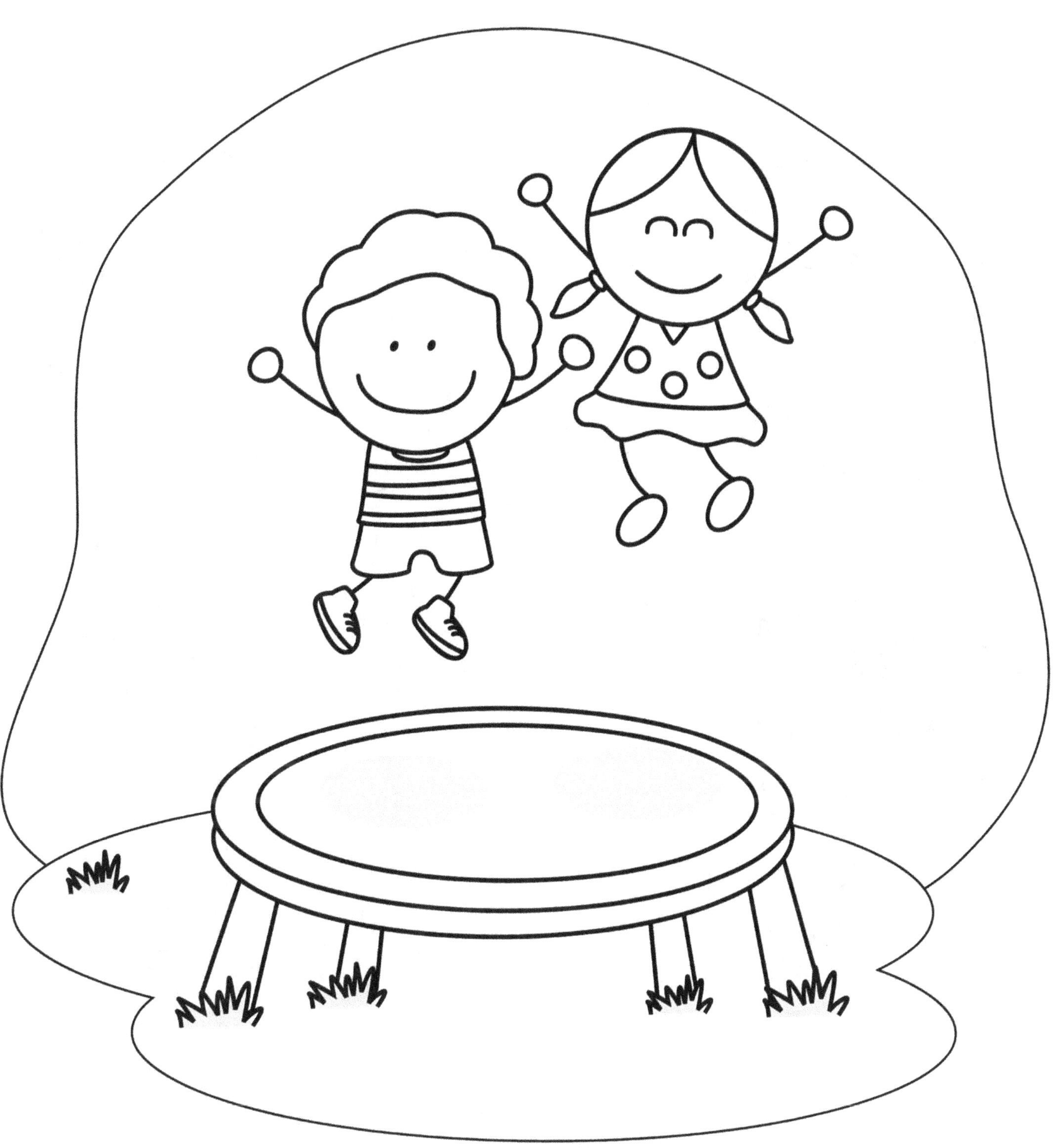

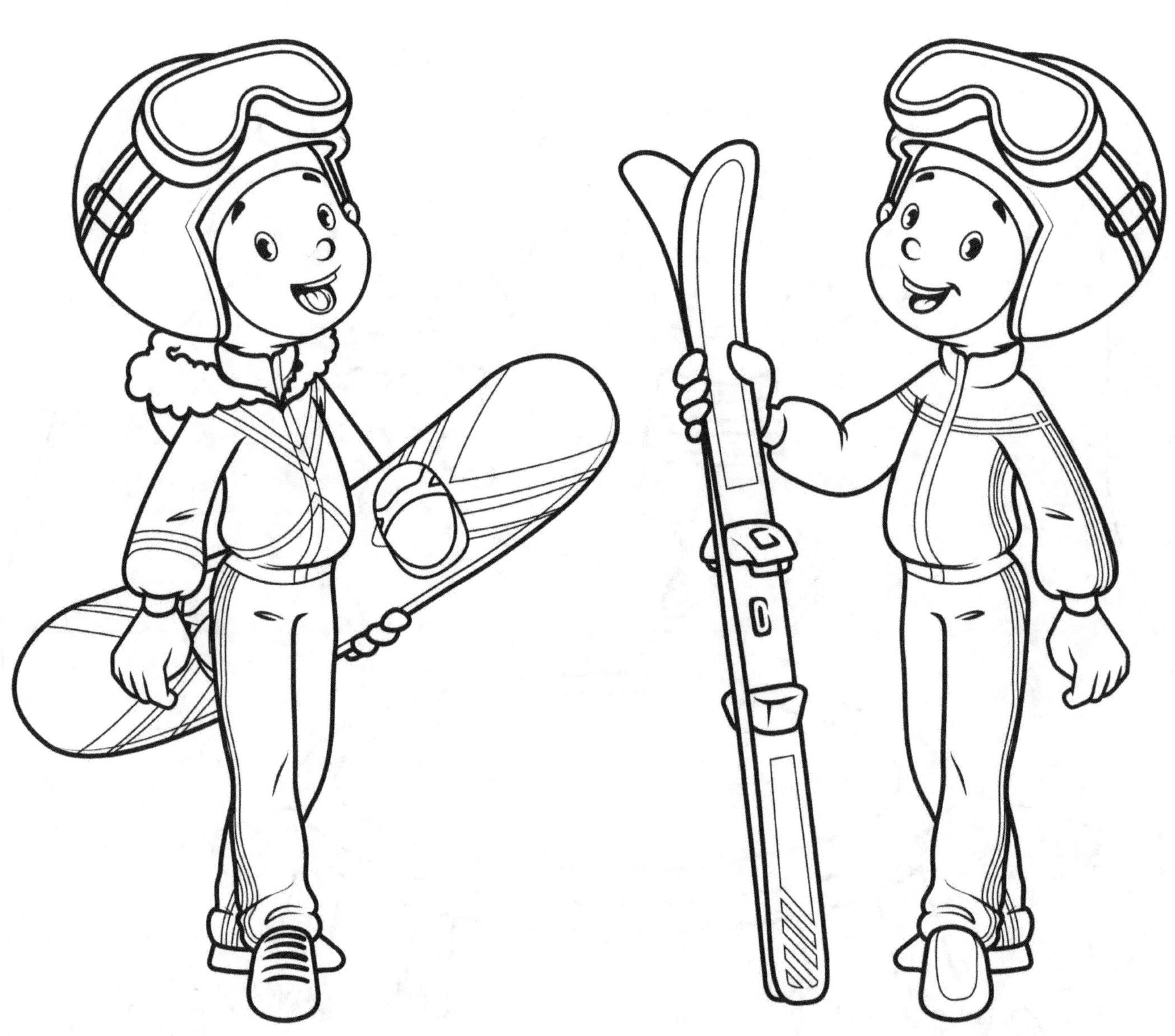

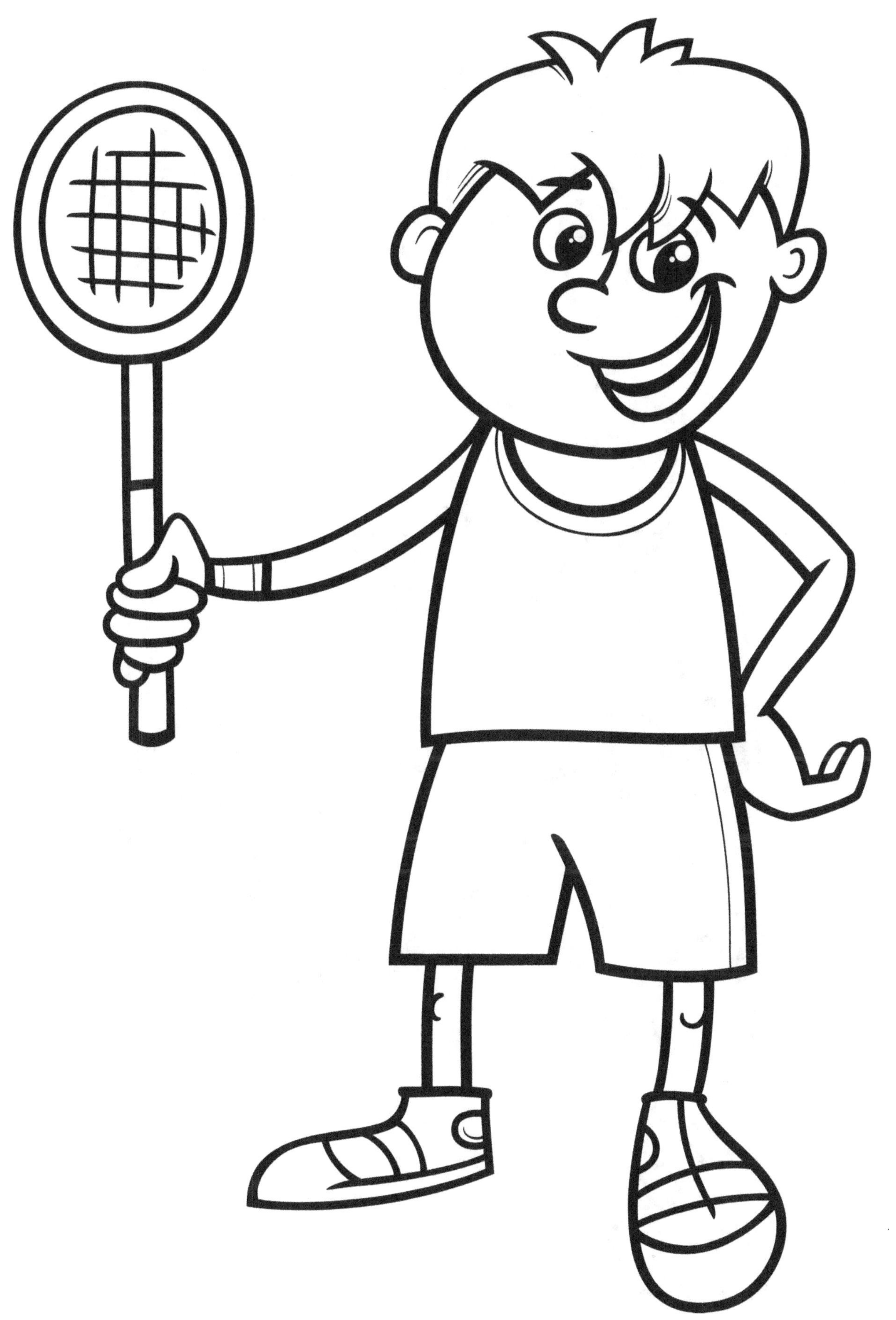

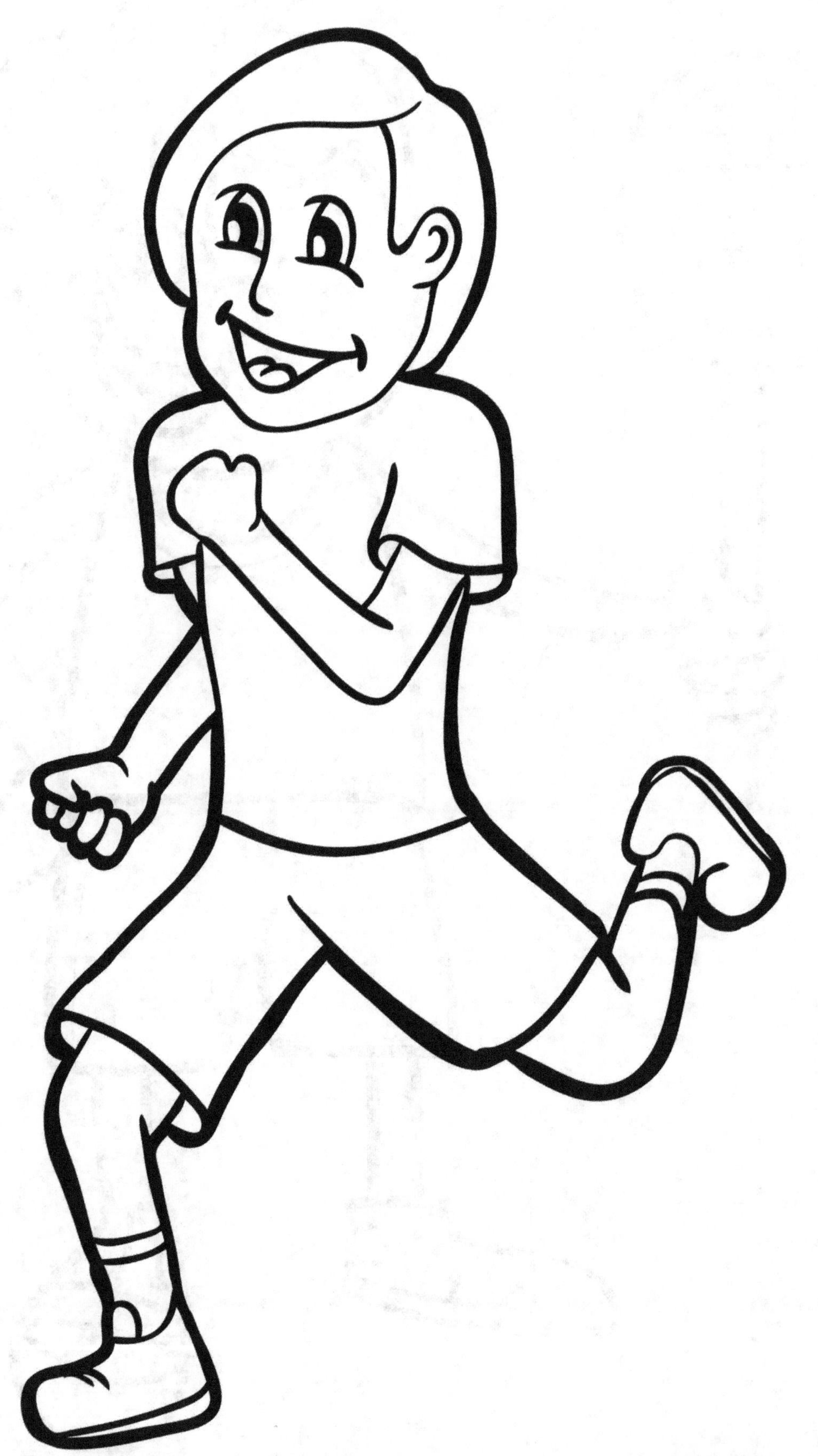

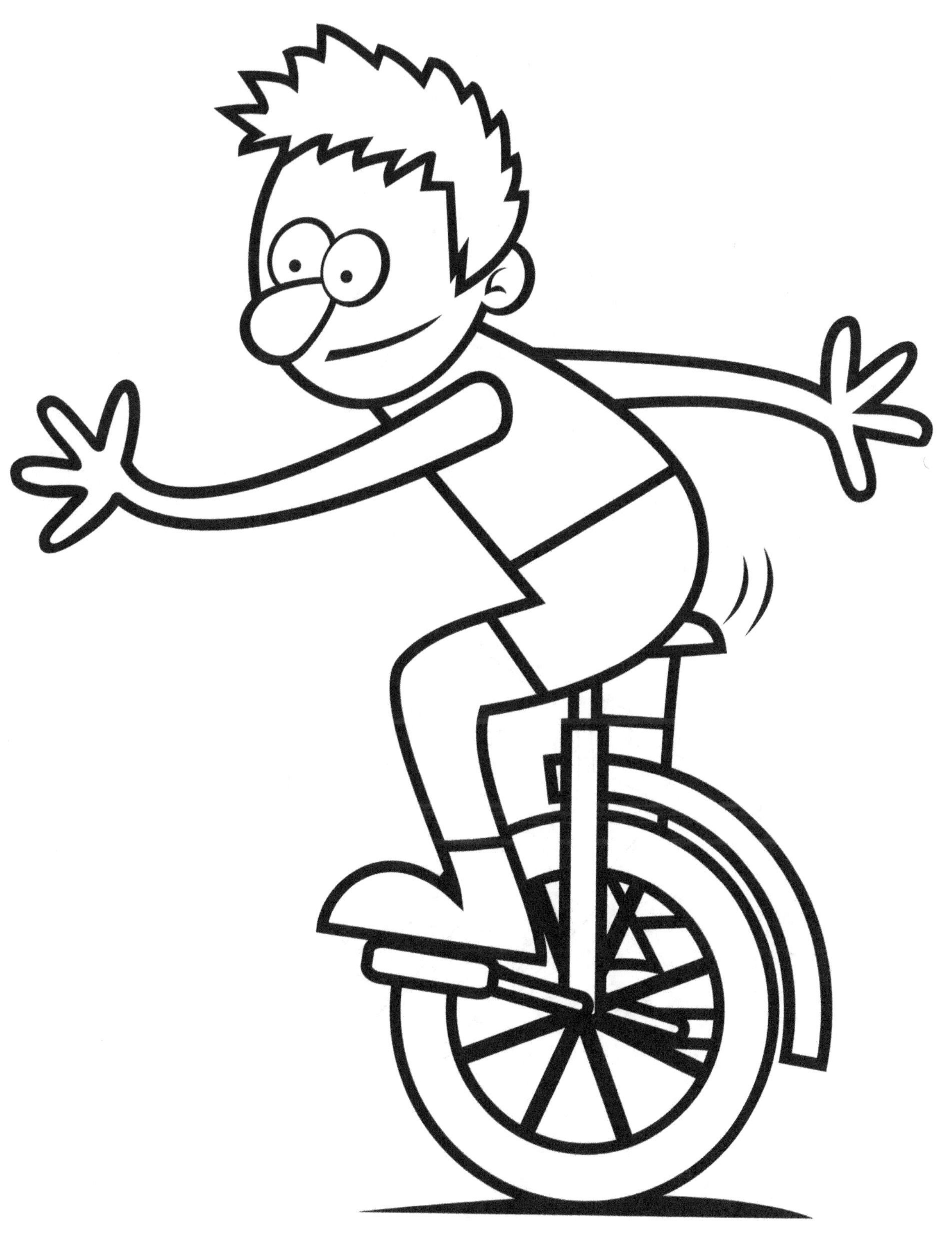

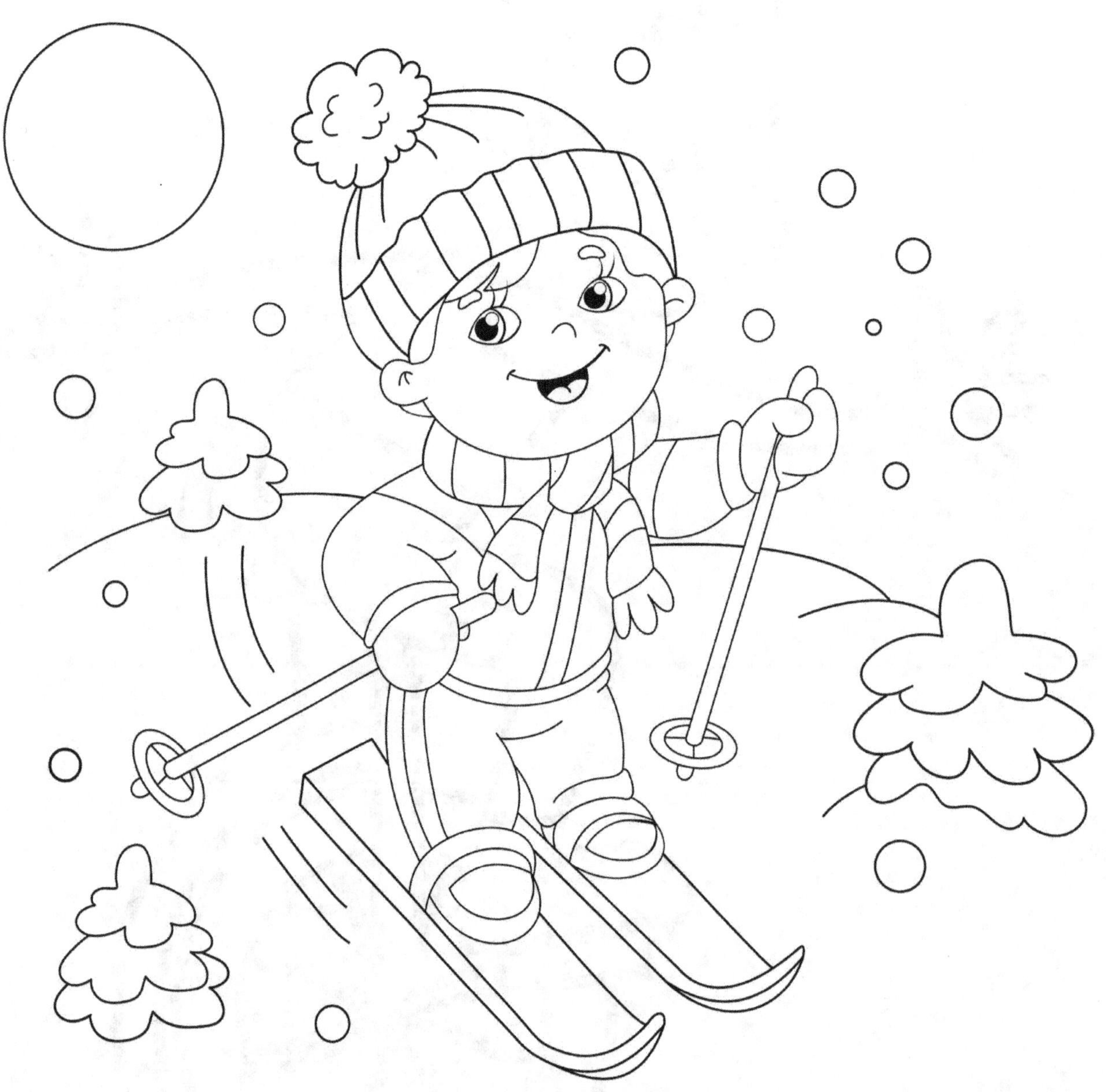

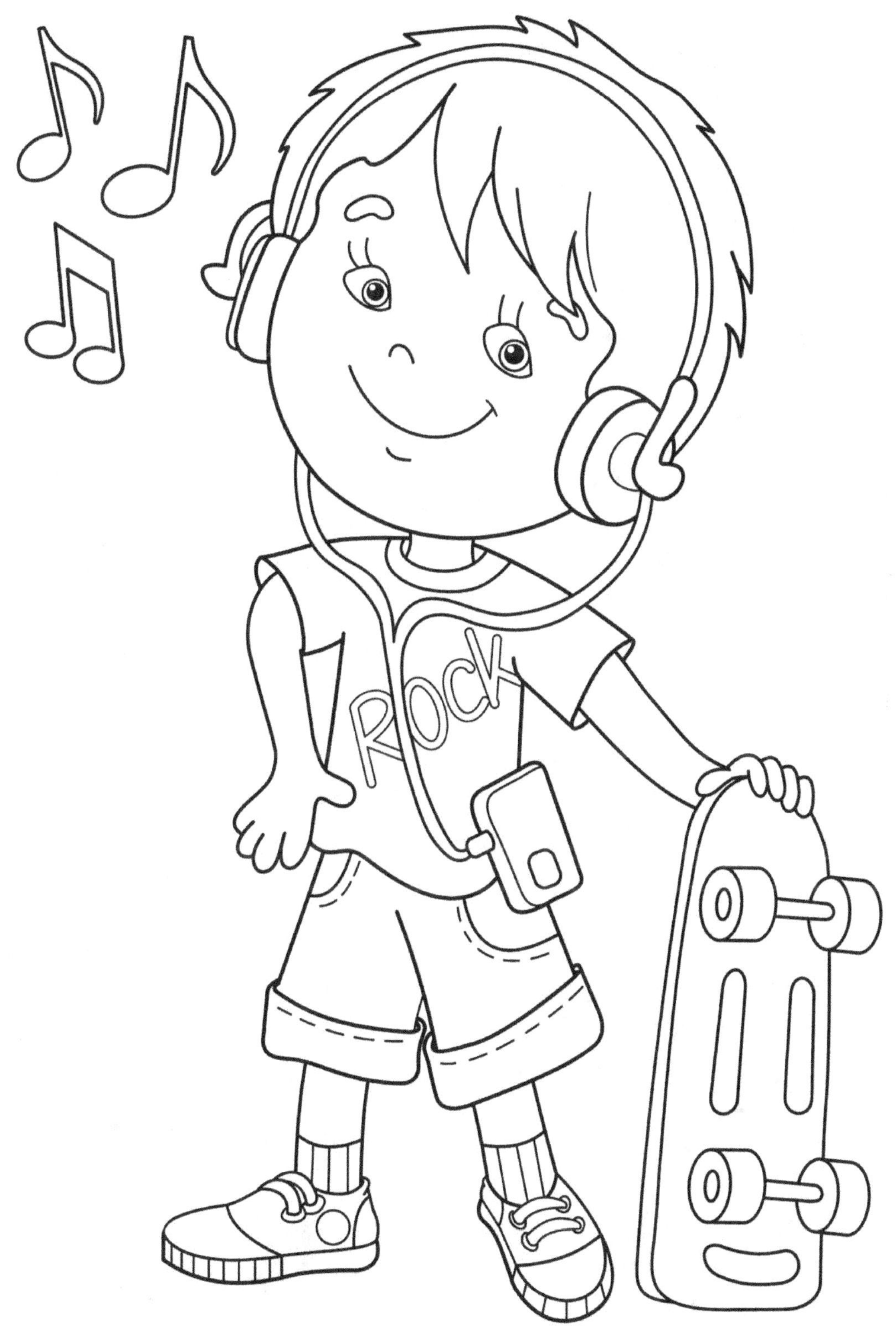ROCK

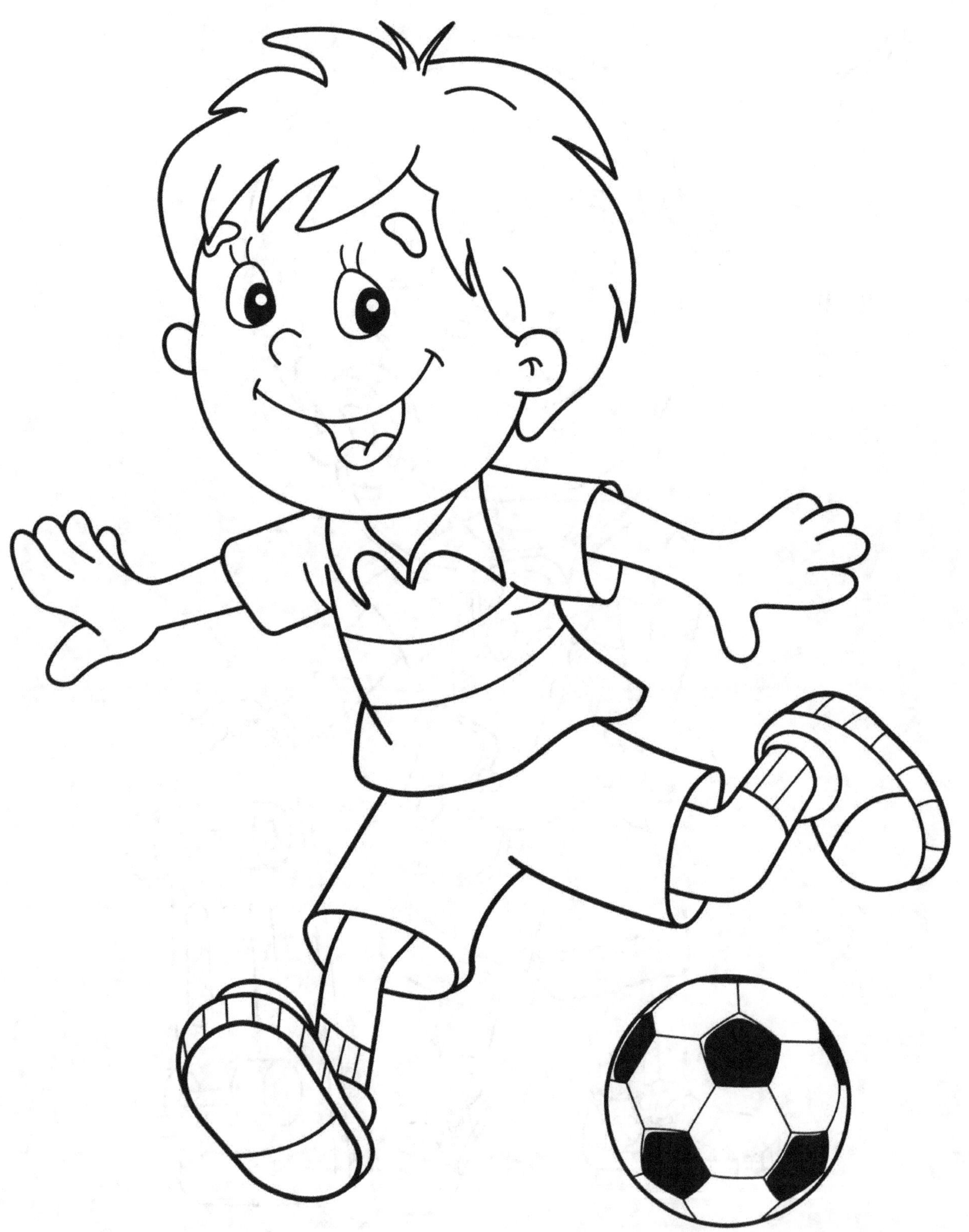